BELLE STARR

Carl R. Green
➤ and ❖
William R. Sanford

ENSLOW PUBLISHERS, INC.

Bloy St. and Ramsey Ave.   P.O. Box 38
Box 777   Aldershot
Hillside, N.J. 07205   Hants GU12 6BP
U.S.A.   U.K.

Library of Congress Cataloging-In-Publication Data

Green, Carl R.
    Belle Starr / Carl R. Green and William R. Sanford.
        p. cm. — (Outlaws and lawmen of the wild west)
    Includes bibliographical references and index.
    Summary: Chronicles the true life story of Belle Starr, as opposed to the myths that have surrounded this famous Western figure.
    ISBN 0-89490-363-2
    1. Starr, Belle, 1848–1889—Juvenile literature. 2. Outlaws—West (U.S.)—Biography—Juvenile literature. 3. West (U.S.)— Biography— Juvenile literature. 4. Frontier and pioneer life—West (U.S.)— Juvenile literature. [1. Starr, Belle, 1848–1889. 2. Robbers and outlaws. 3. West (U.S.)—Biography.] I. Sanford, William R. (William Reynolds), 1927– . II. Title. III. Series: Green, Carl R. Outlaws and lawmen of the wild west.
F594.S8G74 1992
364.1'55'092—dc20
[B]   91-22310
                                                                        CIP
                                                                         AC

Printed in the United States of America

10 9 8 7 6 5 4 3 2 1

Illustration Credits: Archives and Manuscripts Division of the Oklahoma Historical Society, pp. 23, 25, 26, 27, 30, 40, 43, 44; Carl R. Green and William R. Sanford, pp. 7, 15; Library of Congress, pp. 12, 20; Shiloh Museum/Phillip Steele, pp. 17, 18, 32, 33, 34, 39; Shiloh Museum/ Robert G. Winn, p. 10; Western History Collections, University of Oklahoma Library, pp. 6, 36.

Cover Illustration: Library of Congress

CONTENTS

AUTHORS' NOTE

This book tells the true story of the outlaw Belle Starr. Belle was sometimes known as the "Bandit Queen." But her true fame did not begin until after she was killed. That was when the press raced to print stories about her. Some were made up, but others were true. The events described in this book all come from firsthand reports.

1
DALLAS LOVED ITS BANDIT QUEEN

Dallas, Texas, was a boomtown in 1872. It was a railroad center, and money came flowing in. Cattle that once were driven up the long trail to Kansas now moved by rail. The town was proud of its eighteen brick stores and four banks. It also boasted of Belle Starr, its "Bandit Queen."

With her husband on the run from the law, Belle lived well in Dallas. Stolen money paid for her rooms in a good hotel. A maid took care of her children and a groom cared for her horse.

Belle rode sidesaddle to prove that she could be a lady. She also put on a style show when she went riding. Her riding outfit was a tight black jacket and a flowing velvet skirt. Leather boots gleamed with the same high polish as her saddle. A cowboy hat topped with an ostrich feather shaded her eyes. To complete her outfit she buckled on a gunbelt and two loaded pistols.

Riding sidesaddle and dressed in velvet, Belle Starr played at being a fine lady. The sixgun she wears is part of a more famous role—that of Bandit Queen. She was also a hard-living frontier wife, mother, horse thief, and friend of outlaws.

Dallas was a wide-open town, and Belle liked it that way. She spent much of her time in saloons. When Belle went out on the town she wore a leather dress trimmed with beads. At her throat she wore a necklace of rattlesnake rattles. Like the cowboys she drank whiskey and gambled at dice and cards. Then, when the mood hit, she jumped on her horse and galloped through the streets. As she rode she yelled and fired her pistols in the air.

No one tried to stop Belle's wild rides. It would have been risky to do so. Her husband was a wanted man with a price on his head. Some of her best friends were gunslingers. Besides, who cared? Many people in Dallas were proud of their Bandit Queen.

REWARD

 **$10,000**

Will be paid by the State of Missouri for the arrest

DEAD OR ALIVE

of

BELLE STARR

Wanted for Robbery, Murder, Treason and other acts against the peace of the State.

Mich'l K. MacGrath
Secretary of State

This bogus reward poster is part of the myth of the Bandit Queen. Belle may have stolen horses, but she was never guilty of murder or treason. Also, no one would have offered $10,000 for the Starrs. Rewards of that size were only posted for famous outlaws like Jesse James.

2

GROWING UP IN MISSOURI

Belle Starr was born February 5, 1848 on a farm in southwest Missouri. Her parents were John and Elizabeth Shirley. The baby's name at birth was Myra Maybelle Shirley. The family called her May. It was years later that May began calling herself Belle. She took the name Starr from her second husband.

In 1851 John Shirley sold his farm for a good price. He moved his family to the nearby town of Carthage. There he built the Carthage Hotel, a stable, and a blacksmith shop. His buildings soon took up most of one side of the town square. The Shirley family was growing almost as fast as the business. May was John's fourth child, after two boys and a girl. In Carthage, Elizabeth gave birth to three more boys.

May had a happy childhood. By the standards of the time her father was a rich man. That gave her status in the small town. As a girl she was small, dark-haired, and pretty. She also had a hot temper. Her friends said she was ready to fight anyone who crossed her.

Elizabeth had high hopes for May. She sent her to the Carthage Female Academy to learn to be a lady. May was a good student. She studied languages and music as well as reading, writing, and arithmetic. In the evening she showed off by playing the piano at the hotel. Guests spoiled her by giving her gifts.

May's best friend was her older brother Bud. She shared his love of horses and firearms. By the time May was ten she was a fine rider. She and Bud spent many hours riding through the Jasper County hills. Bud also taught her how to handle firearms. May became an expert shot with pistol or rifle.

The Shirley's peaceful life ended in the late 1850s. The problem of slavery turned state against state and friend against friend. Missouri was a slave state, and John Shirley was one of the people who owned slaves. But the free state of Kansas lay only a few miles away. Both sides were soon sending raiders across the border to steal horses and burn towns.

In 1861 the Southern states tried to leave the Union. The North fought to stop them. Men from Jasper County took up arms and joined the rebel army. Missouri became a Civil War battleground.

In July 1861 Union troops won a victory near Carthage. The rebel army was forced out of the state. But the fighting did not end. Men who were loyal to the South formed guerrilla bands. The bands ambushed Union troops and tore up rail lines. To John Shirley the raiders were heroes. Bud shared his father's feelings. He joined Quantrill's Raiders, a band led by William C. Quantrill.

Myra Maybelle Shirley, the young girl who would later become Belle Starr, was a good student and a skilled piano player. She was also a crack shot and a fine rider. During the Civil War she put her skills to use as a spy for Quantrill's Raiders.

May was only fourteen, but she wanted to help. She could not fight, so she became a spy. Her job was to find out what she could about Union forces. How many men did they have? Where were they camped? What kind of guns did they have? She passed these secrets on to the rebels.

Quantrill now led over a thousand men. Young Jim Reed was one of the newest Raiders. Jim, also from Carthage, was May's sweetheart. In August 1862 the Raiders cut railroad lines and won a few small battles. The Union Army struck back, forcing the Raiders to fight for their lives. By December things were too hot for Quantrill. He broke off the action and led his men into Arkansas.

Two months later May made a brave ride to save her brother. Some writers say there is no proof that the ride took place. Others are certain it did. Here is the story.

Early in the new year, Bud came home on leave. While Bud was in Carthage, May went on a scouting trip. Her ride took her to Newtonia, thirty-five miles away. Major Eno of the Union cavalry had his command post there. To her dismay May learned that Eno had sent soldiers to capture Bud. But she was captured before she could ride home to warn him. Eno took a fancy to the pretty young rebel. He took her to the house he used as a headquarters and guarded her himself.

May was not afraid. She stamped her foot and swore at the major. When Eno laughed at her she became even

Quantrill's Raiders lay waste to a western town. The guerrillas swore that they were fighting for the South. More often the rebel cause served as an excuse for an orgy of looting and burning.

angrier. She sat down at the piano and pounded out one loud tune after another. After a while Eno let May go. He was sure she could not beat his men to Carthage.

That was a mistake. May cut across the countryside. With reckless courage she jumped fences and streams. When her horse slowed she lashed it with a whip. The wild ride paid off. May was waiting when Eno's men rode into town. She smiled and greeted the dusty soldiers. "Captain Shirley isn't here," she told them. "He left half an hour ago."

Bud did not escape the next Union trap. In June 1864 a unit of Union soldiers moved into Carthage. They soon learned that Bud and a friend were staying at a house in a nearby town. Moving quickly, they circled the house. Bud was shot and killed as he tried to jump over a fence.

May swore to avenge her brother's death, but there was little she could do. The war was coming to a close. With his son dead, a saddened John Shirley said he was sick of fighting. He sold his property and loaded the family into two covered wagons. May did not want to leave Jim Reed, but she obeyed her father. She drove one of the wagons as the family headed toward Texas. Preston, the oldest boy, already had a farm near Dallas.

3

MARRYING AN OUTLAW

The Shirleys were not the only ones moving. It seemed as though every other house in Carthage was marked G.T.T. The letters stood for *Gone to Texas*.

Dallas was still a small town when May first saw it. Wooden sidewalks lined streets that turned into muddy streams when it rained. Farmers and cowboys bought supplies and looked for fun on Main Street. General stores offered the supplies. Gambling halls and saloons promised a good time.

John Shirley settled in Scyene, southeast of Dallas. He claimed some land above South Mesquite Creek. The fertile black soil was good for growing corn and other crops. Shirley also raised hogs and fast horses. At first the family lived in a cabin. Later they moved into a four-room house, the largest in Scyene. When the creek ran dry May filled barrels of water at the town well. Then she dragged the barrels home on a sled.

By Texas standards May was well educated. As a result she looked down on the town's one-room school. Instead of going to school, she kept busy with housework, caring for her brothers, and tending the garden. For fun she rode her horse along Mesquite Creek. When May stopped to gossip she asked for the latest news from Missouri. Perhaps someone told her about Jesse James and his gang.

In 1866 the James gang robbed a bank of cash and gold coins. The outlaws rode to San Antonio, Texas, to swap the gold for paper money. Far from Missouri,

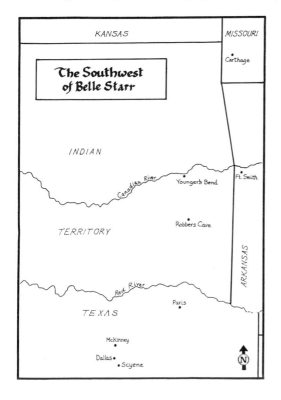

May's family moved to Texas while she was a teenager. It was around Dallas and Fort Smith, Arkansas that May earned fame as the Bandit Queen.

banks in San Antonio would not ask questions about where the gold coins were from. On the way back to Missouri they stopped at the Shirley house. John Shirley was glad to see Jesse James and the four Younger brothers—Jim, Cole, Bob, and John. Shirley was a law-abiding man, but the Youngers were old friends from Missouri.

Some books turn the visit into a romance. The writers claim that Cole Younger was the father of May's first child. It is likely that Cole did admire May's good looks. Many men did. But Cole always denied that he was May's lover. More to the point, May's daughter was not born until two years later.

Jim Reed was the man who made May's heart beat faster. Jim and his family had followed the Shirleys to Texas. May was glad to be united again with her old sweetheart. The courtship moved swiftly. On November 1, 1866 Jim and May were married.

Did John Shirley try to keep the lovers apart? Some writers claim that he did not want May to marry Jim Reed. As they tell the story, Jim and his friends carried Belle off on horseback. Once safely away they stopped for a hasty wedding—still on horseback.

The elopement makes a good story, but the facts do not back it up. The Reeds and the Shirleys were good friends. After the wedding Jim and May moved in with her parents. Jim helped his father-in-law raise hogs and horses.

A year later Jim's mother moved back to Missouri. The young couple went with her. Jim worked the family

May poses with her childhood sweetheart, Jim Reed. It was Reed who first drew May into the outlaw life.

farm at Rich Hill. There, in 1868, May gave birth to a daughter. She named her Rosie Lee, but always spoke of the baby as "my pearl." Soon everyone called the girl Pearl.

Jim grew bored with farm life. He gambled, raced horses, and spent time in the Indian Territory. While there he made friends with Tom Starr. A Cherokee, Tom Starr was the head of a large family that paid little respect to the law.

Trouble seemed to follow Jim Reed. His brother was murdered, so Jim went into Arkansas after the killers and shot them. The killings left him saddled with a murder charge of his own. Jim picked up May and

Pearl, and sought safety with Tom Starr. Arkansas lawmen could not arrest him on Indian lands.

Restless and fearful, Jim next moved his family to the West Coast. It was around this time May began to call herself Belle. In 1871 she gave birth to a son in Los Angeles, California. She named him James Edward. Life was good until Jim was arrested for passing fake money. The police soon found that he was wanted for murder. Jim jumped bail and headed east. Belle, Pearl, and little Eddie followed by stagecoach.

Back in Texas Belle's father gave the Reeds a farm to work. Jim and Belle turned it into a hideout for horse thieves. But Jim still had a price on his head. Leaving the

Jim Reed was May's first husband and the father of her two children. Reed never could settle down to a quiet life as a farmer.

children in Scyene, he and Belle went north to the Indian Territory. There, in the fall of 1873, Jim and some friends tortured and robbed a rich farmer. They escaped with $30,000.

Three months later the law came looking for Jim. He went into hiding, and Belle moved back to her parents' house. She spent part of the time in a Dallas hotel. That was when people began to call her the Bandit Queen. Belle did not mind. She was having a good time spending Jim's stolen money.

The marriage broke up in 1874. Jim had a new girlfriend and a new gang. On April 7 the Reed gang held up the Austin stage. The gunmen robbed the passengers and looted the mail sacks. Stagecoach holdups were new to Texas. A large reward was put up for the capture of the gang.

A lawman named John Morris tracked Jim Reed to Paris, Texas. Morris wanted the reward but he did not want to risk a gunfight. Posing as a friend, Morris talked Jim into a plan "to rob an old man." On the way, they stopped to rest at an inn. Morris pulled his gun while Jim was eating lunch. Jim, who was unarmed, picked up a table and ran toward the lawman. Morris fired. The bullets smashed through the table and hit the outlaw in the chest.

The killing earned Morris a reward of $1,700. It also left Belle a widow.

The Bandit Queen's colorful life was written up in national magazines. Here, the Police Gazette imagines an 1886 scene in which Belle has been set free on bail. The artist took a number of liberties with the facts. By 1886 Belle was no longer this young and pretty.

4
BELLE FALLS IN WITH MORE BAD COMPANY

Little is known of Belle's life in the four years after Jim Reed's death. It is clear that she did not fulfill her mother's hopes that she would become a lady. Although she still dressed well, she looked old for her years. Her hands were roughened by the hard work of farming and keeping house. Her skin was burned by the summer sun and chapped by the winter cold. She spent more time with outlaws than with honest folk.

John Shirley died in 1876. Belle, who was living near Dallas, sold the farm he had given her. She paid for Pearl to go to acting school. Eddie was more of a problem. She loved her son, but the two fought all the time. At last Belle sent him to Missouri to live with his Grammy Reed at Rich Hill.

Belle liked men, and men liked her. For a while she was seen with a Kansas miner named Bruce Younger.

Bruce was an uncle of the Younger brothers, and an old family friend. Another time a rich rancher came to her aid. Belle had been put on trial for burning a store. The rancher saw her in court and liked what he saw. After helping her win the case, he gave Belle a large sum of money.

When Belle married again she chose Tom Starr's son Sam. Belle liked big men and Sam Starr was six feet five inches tall. The handsome Cherokee was also nine years younger than Belle. In 1880 the two joined hands in a tribal wedding.

Belle and Sam claimed a thousand acres of Indian land on the Canadian River. Their farm, with its typical frontier house, was forty miles west of Fort Smith, Arkansas. The house had one room and a lean-to kitchen in back. A sagging front porch shaded the front of the house. Water came from a nearby spring. Belle tried to beautify the inside of her crude house. She bought a flower print fabric and covered the walls with it.

When Belle was settled Pearl came to live with her. The girl was a help in the house and garden. Belle called her farm Younger's Bend. She wrote, "On the Canadian River . . . I hoped to pass the remainder of my life in peace."

That hope soon died. Most of Sam and Belle's friends were outlaws. Younger's Bend became a hideout. The only way in was through a brush-filled canyon. Lookouts watched for any lawman who came their way. The

This photo of the homestead at Younger's Bend was taken after Belle died. During her lifetime the farm was often a hideout for outlaws. Belle did not ride with the gangs, but she did deal in stolen horses.

outlaws also hid in Robber's Cave, a day's ride away. Today the cave is a popular tourist spot.

Belle claimed that Jesse James was her first "guest." In time business was so good she had to build two more cabins. The outlaws stayed busy while they were at Younger's Bend. They stole horses, robbed salesmen, and sold moonshine whiskey to the Indians. Belle sat in on meetings and helped plan new crimes. She also bought and sold stolen horses.

In 1882 Belle's dealings in horses brought the law to Younger's Bend. A U.S. Marshal charged that she and

Sam had stolen a horse. The horse's owner, Pleasant Crane, put the value of the horse at $80. The marshal arrested the couple and took them to jail in Fort Smith.

Belle was no stranger to jails. One story claims that she was first jailed in 1878. If the story is true, Belle so charmed her jailer that he set her free. When she fled he went with her. A few days later she tied him to his horse and sent him back. Pinned to his badge was a note that said he was "unsatisfactory."

At Fort Smith a hearing was held on the horse stealing charge. Pleasant Crane claimed that Belle told him a man named Childs took the horse. But a neighbor swore that he had seen Belle riding the same horse. That was enough for the court. Belle and Sam were ordered to stand trial. They went free on bail after Tom Starr put up the bail money. Belle hired a lawyer to defend them.

The four-day trial took place in 1883. Sam claimed that he was sick with measles at the time of the theft. But no one could pin down the date when measles had broken out. Belle stuck to her story that Childs had the horse. But Childs was not there to back up her story. He had gone off to Texas. When the case went to the jury both Starrs were found guilty.

Belle and Sam had reason to fear a long jail term. Judge Isaac Parker was due to pass sentence on them. Fat and bearded, Parker looked a little like Santa Claus. But he is best known as "the hanging judge." In all, Judge Parker sent eighty-eight men to their death on the gallows.

Judge Isaac Parker was known as "the hanging judge." He earned that title by sending over eighty men to the gallows. When Belle and Sam Starr appeared before him, he let them off with one-year sentences.

For once Parker showed mercy. He could have sent the Starrs to prison for many years. Instead he gave them one-year terms in a Michigan prison. If they stayed out of trouble they could be out in nine months. Many stories are told of Belle spending time in one jail or another. Her stay in Michigan, however, is the only jail term for which records exist.

Belle and Sam had a second stroke of luck. The house of correction they were sent to tried to help its inmates. At first Belle was put to work weaving cane bottoms for chairs. But she soon caught the warden's eye. He put her

The Fort Smith, Arkansas courthouse as it looked in the early 1900s. Judge Isaac Parker handed down a number of his death sentences in this imposing building. It was also in Fort Smith that Belle was convicted of horse theft.

to work in his office and let her teach music to his children. In her spare time Belle began writing a love story. Sam's life was harder. He spent the long days breaking rocks with a sledgehammer.

The Starrs were set free at the end of nine months. Belle was anxious to return to Younger's Bend. There were crops to plant and a house to care for. Most of all she missed her children, who had been staying with trusted friends. Before going to prison she had written to Pearl to describe their future. In the letter she said, "We will have Eddie with us and will be as gay and happy as the birds. . . . "

Belle and her family lived in this crude cabin at Younger's Bend. Belle and Pearl did their cooking in the lean-to kitchen at the back of the cabin. At night visiting outlaws met on the porch to swap tall tales and plan new crimes.

5
BELLE TURNS OVER A NEW LEAF

With their prison term ended Belle and Sam headed home. On the way they picked up Pearl and Mabel Harrison. Mabel was an orphan who had become Pearl's best friend. Back at Younger's Bend Belle fixed up the house. Sam put in the spring crops.

Belle did not like to cook, so the girls fixed the meals. For special days Belle liked to whip up a batch of sugar candy. One of those times was when Eddie came home. For the first time in years Belle had both children with her. Another special day was when a piano arrived at Younger's Bend. Belle banged out church hymns and songs such as "Listen to the Mockingbird." Pearl and Eddie took lessons, but neither showed much musical talent.

The peaceful times did not last. In late 1885 Sam was accused of robbing a store and post office. With the law on his trail he went into hiding. Indian police often came to Younger's Bend to look for him. Only when the coast was clear could Sam visit Belle and the children.

Belle was having troubles of her own. Three months after Sam left she was accused of stealing horses again. Belle went to Fort Smith and entered a not guilty plea. While she was free on bail she was charged with taking part in a robbery. Those charges were soon dropped.

In the fall Belle was tried on the latest horse stealing charge. She produced a witness who swore that Belle had paid a stranger $50 for the horse. The jury believed the witness. Although she won her case Belle could not relax. Word soon reached her that Sam had been shot.

Feeling safe for the moment, Sam had gone riding on Venus, Belle's best horse. As luck would have it he ran into a four-man posse. Frank West, an old enemy, opened fire without warning. One bullet killed Venus and another grazed Sam's head. The bloody wound looked worse than it was. After two of the men left to find a wagon Sam grabbed a rifle. Swiftly he disarmed his guards. Then he escaped on one of their horses.

Belle nursed Sam at his brother's house. As he healed she argued that he should give himself up. She told Sam the Indian police would kill him if they found him. Sam saw that she had a point. He turned himself in to a lawman who took him to Fort Smith. Belle rode behind the two men, twin pistols strapped to her waist. After Sam was charged she put up his bail.

Belle often strapped on a pair of six-guns to complete her outfit. Although she was an expert shot, she did not go out of her way to use her pistols. When Sam Starr was in jail, she simply bailed him out instead of leading a jailbreak.

All was calm until a week before Christmas. The Starrs went to a dance at a neighbor's house. Belle played the organ for the dancing. During the party someone ran in to tell Sam that Frank West was outside. Sam found West and accused him of killing Venus. In the next instant the two men were reaching for their guns. Sam fired first; West, a second later. When the smoke cleared both of them were dead.

Belle held Sam's head in her lap and cursed Frank West. She had loved this outlaw husband. But that was not her only loss. Sam's death also meant that she could not keep her farm. Only Cherokees could live on Cherokee land. Belle would have to move unless she wed another Indian.

Finding a new man was not hard for Belle. Some stories claim she had been seeing other men all this time. One lover may have been John Middleton. Gossip says that Belle was ready to run off with him. If so, Sam had spoiled the plan by showing up before they could leave. No one knows what took place next. The only certainty is that Middleton's body was found a few days later.

Other stories say Belle loved an Indian outlaw named Blue Duck. Blue Duck, it seems, lost his money in a gambling hall. Belle showed up there the next night. Pistol in hand, she took back the money Blue Duck had lost. As she left someone said she had taken too much. "Come to my farm and get it," she yelled back. No one took her up on the offer.

A photo of Belle and Blue Duck does exist. Most experts say she posed at the request of friends. Being seen with her, they thought, might help Blue Duck. At the time he was on trial for murder.

In early 1887 Belle invited Tom Starr's adopted son to move in with her. At twenty-four, Bill July was fifteen years younger than Belle. With July by her side Belle's farm was safe. She turned over a new leaf at the same time. She let everyone know that outlaws were no longer welcome at Younger's Bend.

Pearl was now nineteen and argued with Belle all the time. For one thing she disliked Bill July. Belle did not like it when Pearl called Bill a lazy horse thief. But it was Pearl's boyfriends who caused the most trouble. One young man had gone so far as to ask for Pearl's hand. Belle turned him down. She did not want her daughter to marry a poor man. That was too much for Pearl. She

Belle poses with a handcuffed Blue Duck. Was Blue Duck her lover or only an outlaw in need of a friend? Like so much in Belle's life, no one can say for sure. What is certain is that Belle liked handsome young men.

Pearl Starr was born with Belle's looks and spirit. Mother and daughter had many fights, but they cared deeply for each other. After Belle's death Pearl made enough money to furnish this elegant Ft. Smith home. She married several times and died in Arizona in 1925.

left home and ended up living with her grandmother in Arkansas. Late in the year she gave birth to a daughter she named Flossie.

Pearl was only one of Belle's worries. Bill July was jailed for stealing a horse, but Belle refused to help him. When he got out on bail she gave him a public scolding. Young Eddie was also in and out of trouble. In the summer of 1888 he and Mose Perryman came to blows over a stolen horse. Mose shot Eddie in the head.

Belle brought her wounded son back to the farm. When Pearl heard about the shooting she came home to nurse him. As Eddie's wound healed he and Belle argued more and more. After one quarrel Belle told the village postmaster not to give Eddie her mail. She soon learned that Eddie had a temper of his own. He took his mother's letters at gunpoint.

Belle found out about the stolen letters. She lashed Eddie with a whip. Later she again used a whip on him when he abused her horse. That was too much for Eddie. He moved out. Belle never saw him again.

Eddie Reed was the second of Belle's two children. Often in trouble with the law, he surprised his friends by becoming a deputy marshal. Eddie was killed in 1896 when he tried to arrest two men for selling whiskey.

6

THE DEATH OF
THE BANDIT QUEEN

Belle turned forty in 1888. She looked older. Hard living had streaked her black hair with gray. Her skin was burned by sun and wind to a leathery brown. Her nose stuck out as sharp as an eagle's beak. People whispered that she looked like an Indian.

Even so, men turned to stare when Belle rode by. Proud of her small feet, she wore only the finest boots. When she went riding she carried "my baby." "Baby" was a Colt .45 pistol.

Belle held fast to what was left of her ladylike ways. A shelf in her cabin held her father's books. She played the piano and organ. Some women smoked cigars when they gambled in the saloons. Belle liked to gamble, but she never smoked cigars.

One day, as she was riding near Fort Smith, her hat blew off. A cowboy saw the hat but refused to chase it.

The two sides of Belle Starr show up in this 1887 portrait. The lady in Belle insisted that she put on a stylish dress. But her gunslinger side felt undressed without the twin pistols.

Belle drew her Colt and ordered him to pick it up. The surprised cowboy obeyed. Belle took the hat and put it on. Then she said, "The next time a *lady* asks you to pick up her hat, do as she tells you."

Back at the farm Belle's neighbors had mixed feelings about her. Some liked her, others feared her. For her part Belle thought most women were boring. When one came to call she would grab a book and hide until the visitor left. But if Belle liked someone, she could be kind and helpful. When friends were sick she often showed up to help with the nursing.

This was the "new" Belle. Outlaws were not allowed to stay at her farm. Her neighbors no longer lost their stock to her "guests." When friends came by Belle showed them a letter from Robert Owen, the local Indian Agent. Owen had written to say that a complaint against Belle had been dropped. He praised her for keeping "bad characters" away from Younger's Bend.

If Belle was changing, so was the Indian Territory. The Indians now rented rich bottom land to settlers. Poor farmers from the South snapped up the land. The rent was one-fourth of the cotton and corn the tenants raised.

Belle was renting parcels of her own land. One of her would-be tenants was Edgar Watson. Watson knew the black soil would grow good crops. Also, as Belle's tenant, he would not have to take out a new lease each year.

The deal went sour after Belle became friends with Watson's wife. Mrs. Watson told Belle about her husband's past. She said that Watson was wanted on a Florida murder charge. That upset Belle. She had been friends with dozens of bad men in her day. But now she was trying to go straight.

Belle offered to return Watson's rent money. Watson refused to take it. Next, Belle sent the money back in a letter. She also wrote that someone else was taking over the farm. Watson was just as stubborn. He scared the new tenant into backing out of the deal.

That was too much for Belle. She warned Watson that she knew his secret and ordered him to clear out. Watson did not argue with her. When she was done he climbed on his horse and rode away. Pearl watched him leave and urged her mother to be careful. Belle only laughed.

On February 2, 1889 Bill July saddled up to ride to Fort Smith. He was due there to face the old horse stealing charge. Belle rode the ten miles to King Creek with him. She had a bill to pay at the store there. Then the two rode on to spend the night with friends. In the morning Bill went on to Fort Smith. Belle turned back to her farm.

By midday she was eating lunch at King Creek. The store owner asked her why she looked so gloomy. Belle said she feared that someone would try to kill her.

Belle's next stop was at Jackson Rowe's house. She did not see Edgar Watson leave the house as she came up the road. When she reached the porch Belle stopped to chat. After eating a piece of cornbread she asked

Bill July, a young horse thief, became Belle's third husband in 1887. Bill, the adopted son of Tom Starr, also went by the name of Jim July Starr. He died in a shootout with lawmen the year after Belle was killed.

about her son. Eddie was living with the Rowes, but he had gone off to see a friend.

When Belle left she turned into the muddy lane that led to the river. She did not see the man hiding behind a fence. Belle was only twenty feet away when he fired a shotgun. Buckshot tore into her back and neck. She fell from her horse and splashed into the mud. As she tried to rise the killer ran up and fired again.

Down at the river a neighbor saw Belle's horse dash by. He raced up the road and found her body. By the time he brought Pearl to the spot it was too late. Belle Starr was dead.

The funeral was held three days later. Neighbor women dressed Belle in her best riding clothes. As a final

BELLE STARR
Born in Carthage Mo.
FEB 5, 1848.
DIED
Feb 3, 1889.

hed not for her the bitter tear,
Nor give the heart to vain regret;
'Tis but the casket that lies here,
The gem that filled it sparkles yet.

The tombstone Pearl ordered for Belle Starr says nothing about her outlaw life. Clearly, Pearl did not think of her mother as the Bandit Queen. She also guessed wrong on Belle's birthplace. The Shirleys did not move to Carthage until after Belle was born.

touch Pearl placed her mother's pistol in her hand. Some Indian friends lowered the pine coffin into a grave near the river.

After the grave was closed July pulled a gun. He accused Watson of killing Belle. A court hearing was held but there was no proof that Watson was the killer. Guilty or not, Watson soon packed up and left. He knew July would kill him if he stayed.

Despite everything, Pearl loved her mother. She ordered a tombstone for Belle's grave. The poem she chose to be carved on the stone reads:

> *Shed not for her the bitter tear,*
> *Nor give the heart to vain regret;*
> *'Tis but the casket that lies here,*
> *The gem that filled it sparkles yet.*

7
THE LEGEND OF THE BANDIT QUEEN

The murder of Belle Starr was front-page news. To people eager to know more about the Bandit Queen, the story made good reading. The report in *The New York Times* said Belle was:

> . . . *the most desperate woman that ever figured on the borders. She married Cole Younger . . . but left him and joined a band of outlaws that operated in the Indian Territory. She had been arrested for murder and robbery a score of times, but always managed to escape.*

The paper spelled her name right. None of the other "facts" were true.

Next a reporter named Alton Meyers cashed in on Belle's fame. Meyers did not check his facts either. He rushed into print with *Bella Starr, the Bandit Queen, or the Female Jesse James.* After that the myths piled up quickly. A few examples:

Myth: Belle Starr rode with Quantrill's Raiders during the Civil War. *In fact,* only two women rode with Quantrill. Belle was not one of them.

Myth: Belle Starr would just as soon kill a man as look at him. *In fact,* Belle never killed anyone. She threatened to kill a few, but never pulled the trigger on them.

Myth: Like Jesse James, Belle was the leader of an outlaw gang. *In fact,* Belle was never part of a gang. She

Tall maples shade the tiny schoolhouse at Younger's Bend. Local stories say that Belle Starr planted these trees. As with much of her life, it is hard to know the truth of these stories.

Belle Starr's grave lies close to her cabin at Younger's Bend. Within a year of her death someone had stolen her pistol and jewelry from her coffin. Pearl added the stonework to prevent further grave robberies.

did make money buying and selling stolen horses. She also took money from the outlaws who stayed with her.

Today the myths live on in books, films, and songs. Belle is always billed as the "Bandit Queen." That title is the biggest myth of all. The West never had a true Bandit Queen. Belle, however, was the closest those lawless times could offer.

GLOSSARY

bail—Money paid to a court to guarantee the return of a suspect for trial.

Civil War—The war between the North and South, 1861–1865.

gallows—The platform on which a convicted criminal is hanged.

guerrillas—Small, fast-moving military forces that operate outside the normal rules of warfare.

gunslingers—Outlaws and lawmen of the Wild West who settled arguments with their pistols.

Indian Agent—A federal worker who has the job of making sure that the Indians in an area are treated fairly.

Indian Territory—An area set aside for Indian tribes forced to leave their own land. The Indian Territory Belle Starr lived in is now part of Oklahoma.

jury—A group of people sworn to judge the facts and arrive at a decision in a court case.

myth—A story that many people believe, but which is almost always untrue.

posse—A group of citizens who join with law enforcement officers to aid in the capture of outlaws.

Quantrill's Raiders—A band of Southern guerrillas led by William Quantrill. The Raiders fought against Union forces in Missouri.

Union—The name given to the Northern states that fought against the South during the Civil War.

MORE GOOD READING ABOUT BELLE STARR

Breihan, Carl W. with Charles A. Rosamond. *The Bandit Belle*. Superior, Wisc.: Superior Publishing Company, 1970, pp. 8–17.

Drago, Harry. *Outlaws on Horseback*. New York: Dodd, Mead & Co., 1964, pp. 90–113.

Hicks, Edwin. *Belle Starr and Her Pearl*. St. Louis, Mo.: Pioneer Press, 1963.

Morgan, Speer. *Belle Starr*. New York: Little, Brown and Company, 1979. [A novel.]

Rascoe, Burton. *Belle Starr, the "Bandit Queen."* New York: Random House, 1941.

Shirley, Glenn. *Belle Starr and Her Times; the Literature, the Facts, and the Legends*. Norman, Okla.: University of Oklahoma Press, 1982.

Steele, Phillip W. *Starr Tracks: Belle and Pearl Starr*. Gretna, La.: Pelican, 1989.

Wellman, Paul. "A Brushwood Courtesan," *A Dynasty of Western Outlaws*. New York: Bonanza Books, 1961, pp. 130–157.

INDEX